The History of Tree Roots

The History of Tree Roots

poems by

Phillip Howerton

Preface by Adam Davis

Golden Antelope Press
715 E. McPherson
Kirksville, Missouri 63501
2015

ISBN   978-1-936135-18-9 (1-936135-18-3)

Library of Congress Control Number: 2015956572

Published by:
Golden Antelope Press
715 E. McPherson
Kirksville, Missouri 63501

Available at:
Golden Antelope Press
715 E. McPherson
Kirksville, Missouri, 63501
Phone: (660) 665-0273
http://www.naciketas-press.com
Email: ndelmoni@gmail.com

Several poems in this collection have been previously published. The author wishes to thank the editors of the following publications for granting permission for the poems to be reprinted here.

Big Muddy: A Journal of the Mississippi River Valley
Black Bough
Brussels Sprout
Cantos: A Literary and Arts Journal
Cave Region Review
The Chaffin Journal
The Christian Science Monitor
Elder Mountain: A Journal of Ozarks Studies
EAPSU Online
The Foliate Oak
Frogpond
Hard Row to Hoe
The Hurricane Review
The Journal of Kentucky Studies
The Midwest Quarterly
Pegasus
Plainsongs
Red Rock Review
River Oak Review
Slant: A Journal of Poetry
South Carolina Review
The Ozarks Mountaineer
Timber Creek Review
Yonder Mountain: An Ozarks Anthology

To my mother and father
and their sense of place

"The poem is important, but
not more than the people
whose survival it serves"
—Wendell Berry

Contents

Preface

There's a pastoral tradition in American poetry, to be sure. But Frost, while taking a granite-eyed view of nature, sometimes tipped his carefully-arranged cards and let his years at Dartmouth and Harvard show. Not that there's anything wrong with an elite education, but it did somewhat spoil the self-portrait he was painting. He could be pretentious, or at least his overt and explicit philosophizing would trouble a dialect coach. Moreover, the land itself suffered even in domestic travel: his New England was always too settled to map onto the Ozark experience. This is not a place of mossy stone walls and centuries-old fruit groves. The snow doesn't last as long as the withering hot spells and you walk through the woods knowing there are things out here that wonder what you taste like. The soil here is so thin you can scratch down to the karst with a pocketknife. And the buildings tend towards the ramshackle, their piers and pilings shallow too. The stone age ended here not much over a century and a half back. We still seek our poetic voice.

James Whitcomb Riley is at least geographically nearer. He cultivated in an increasingly urban America a certain bittersweet nostalgia for a vanishing rural life. The past by its nature is of course always vanishing, always just out of reach, and always painful because it was once ours, or nearly ours, or belonged to someone who was ours and is now gone. At his best, he was a sort of white Uncle Remus. More often, he came near the rural equivalent of blackface: "An' the Gobble-uns 'at gits you Ef-you-Don't-Watch-Out!"

Edgar Guest, British-born adopted son of the quaint, old-fashioned city of Detroit, saw that dividing line and ran over and past it, giggling. Hasn't been seen or heard of since. "It takes a heap o' livin'..." Oh criminy. Dorothy Parker's couplet is better than anything he wrote: "I'd rather flunk my Wasserman test/ Than read a poem by Edgar Guest." His full-on, smarmy sentimentality was of course a goldmine, perhaps precisely because even those who thought of it as poetry didn't take it as seriously as one takes real poetry. Real poetry hurts.

Although he takes us back to the East Coast, Edwin Arlington Robinson was serious stuff. "Mr. Flood's Party" and "Miniver Cheevy" are about isolation and silent suffering, which he located in rural and smalltown life. His poems are infused with tragic awareness that in this expanding universe, the arrow of time points one way and one way only. This is the mood of Phillip Howerton's first collection, now in your hands. Time is never kind. Or unkind. It just is. And does.

Howerton writes at some remove from, and among the relics of, a hardscrabble life. A family photo from 1919 sets the tone: a stoic clutch of workworn people, and yet there are two young men – boys really — struggling to suppress their grins. Is it because they do not know what pain lies ahead? Or would not believe it if they did? Do they not know that here at their beginning, they are already someone's distant past?

Perhaps one of those two is the old bachelor we meet a bit later, everything behind him in what were for many of us heady days of endless possibilities, before November 1963. His external silence, his solitude, his isolation mask an inner talkativeness, but it's recursive, returning to the fields of France a lifetime ago and an ocean away.

It is a thorny life where every bucket of water was laboriously drawn, every serving of green beans taken from a jar that I've heard calculated at something like an hour's labor for a big man's mouthful. This writer knows the sound of the waterbucket rising up a narrow wellpipe (not the iconic masonry cylinder with the quaint roof), and the bucket itself — not the old oaken thing of nostalgia but —

> a section of slim stove pipe,
> But crimped and tapered at both ends
> Dull gray and galvanized

This is something good teachers of drawing insist on: depict what you see, not what you expect to see, or think your audience expects to see. It inspires trust in the report. This bucket is ugly, awkward. It feels improvised, as so much in that life often was. It was an it'll-do life. This contraption brings something elemental and necessary from deep down, and it delivers.

Work is hard. Sawmills are understood to be places of ear-rending noise, memorably miserable textures — sawdust and grit stuck on one's sweaty forearms (but it is also a place of intoxicating odors), and the never-remote possibility of horrific mutilation. Off in the house, a woman shudders each time she hears the screech of blade ripping through a few centuries of oak — has it pulled her son or her husband in this time? If it hasn't yet, sooner or later, this or something else these people lean into will devour them.

But it can take a while, and until it does, you take the shape your experiences knock you into. Before high fructose corn syrup, this level of life left a person angular in body, and in other ways too. These people squint through round specs probably better suited to their budgets than to their visual needs, but one keeps squinting. One accumulates damage, one endures. "A Shelf of Old Hammers" calmly observes a collection of deliberate and dignified objects that have taken and given beatings; the metaphor is artfully unspoken: the world leaves marks on us, and we return the favor, in our little way. The old tools are one with a thing every rural Missourian knows, and with which we meet in both poem and photograph, the red cedar that roots itself in the very rock and can writhe its slow way through a thousand years of tough uselessness.

Yes, even the botany is hard. Empirical. The mayapple, which one eats at need. The multiflora and the sumac which mark failure, desertion, despair — the abandonment of a field. A out-of-place pear tree marks the spot where once an orchard stood. A stand of non-native white poplars also remembers a vanished homestead — whose owner perhaps longed for something long gone and far away as well.

Howerton looks about and reads the landscape, which bears testimony to human labor even when depopulated — a string of silvered fenceposts strung along the edge of a feral field calls to his mind the callused hands that hung the barbed wire and pounded every staple. He sees strata, as an archaeologist might: the wooden posts began to be replaced at some point with steel, and that represented a kind of surrender. When the things you work with must be made far away and bought with scarce cash, that was the beginning of the end. One wouldn't have to replace fenceposts much longer.

It is not all elegy. We encounter spirit-animals, totems of a woodsy childhood: crow, grasshopper, spider, skunk, coonhound and possum, squirrel and snake, all observed minutely, known intimately, by their tracks and twitches, by their spoor and sign. The rain crow can say what weather's coming. Howerton shrugs off the authoritative claim that the call of the whippoorwill announced death. "We welcomed it/ when it came to call at dusk."

This was a life that was almost gone by the time of my own suburban boyhood, and the nursing homes and estate sales which figure in some of these lyrics point to the gone-ness of this world. Few things are sadder than a farm auction, and the poet notes his father's poignant attempts to rescue a few of their neighbors' keepsakes, and above all to pass them along with the stories of their previous owners' lives still attached. But the logic which dooms the effort is painfully obvious. Like dry leaves before the autumn blast, so are the generations of men. And thus an old lady's color-box (sold by her children when she and her possessions "had become [...] too much to manage"):

> [...] eccentric petals
> lie gray and blue smatterings
> of a sky she knew was falling.

The country store is mentioned. There were a few left, not long ago, and one of my students recently did a marvelous oral history of one her family had operated for decades, and revealed the degree to which it had been the center of the community — more so than the church. The institution is as gone as the life in which it made sense. It is treated like one of these elderly, with the inevitable grim diagnosis. In another poem, a convenience store now mars the dry land, and one of its operatives, in stupidity or callous indifference, flicks a lit cigarette into the tindery grass.

It's a strangely depopulated weedscape. The academic notes, almost reflexively, the lack of women, of Black people and Indians. But then, there's precious near nobody here, really. A few very old people. Not even Howerton appears onstage much, except as the person writing the lines of poetry. There is very little interiority.

Which takes us to the central concern of the collection: people are places, places are people. They appear, disappear and go to pieces together. There is no "I" and "it."

One rather unusually talky poem expresses an almost prim contempt for a certain kind of outsider, a "rural correspondent" whose foolishness includes cutting hedge-trees for firewood and planting a garden too near a walnut tree, along with graver offenses:

> [He] Admires what folks don't want to share,
> Advertises what they wish to keep to themselves [...]
> Tramps across unmarked graves of the heart,
> Taps old ghosts on the shoulder...

He doesn't get it.

There's annoyance too with the picturesque and commodified. That sort of person doesn't get it either, and in fact, falsifies it: cross-cut saws made into decorations and painted with idealized images of a past that never was, old mailboxes stuffed with flowers. A more detached tone accompanies his view of those who desert the already moribund villages in the winter for their "real homes." He offers no reproach, because there's little left for the snowbirds to abandon, since the railroads came, and then they left, taking with them all the timber and all the youngfolk. As John Prine sang about the place "where Paradise lay," it may not in fact have been much of a paradise, but it was what we had.

Past the midpoint, the downward arc of the collection carries us through the death of the poet's father, who leaves the final bits and pieces to be sorted and settled — and in a requiem poem, Howerton recalls how good the older man had been at identifying and contextualizing the scraps of a gone life, grubbed out of the dirt by the boys. Shards of metal, lengths of chain, he could identify and place on long-obsolete farm equipment. And this is what Howerton's doing. It's more purposeful than a mere lament, an *ubi sunt*. Holding things up to the light, he ponders, "what was it? What did it do?" And Frost, yes, he asked what we are to make of a diminished thing. An earlier poet — strange to think, also a Missourian — talked of shoring fragments up against his ruins. A still older one held up a mysterious object of his own and asked "whom does it serve?" Something can be rescued — the poet continues to work at a bench he built with lumber salvaged from his father's barn.

If there's a single governing idea here, it's that the connection of thing with idea, with meaning, with feeling, is a distinctively human operation. The connection is forged in painful experience, and it is both precious and doomed. But like the plant that gives one of the central poems its name, *sanguinaria canadenis* — this past provides life:

> [...] throbbing from root tip
> To leaf tip with blood
> Drawn from the thin soil
> To which it clings.

Adam Brooke Davis
Truman State University

One: Beyond the Image

The History of Tree Roots

My ancestors settled on these banks
perhaps by accident, delivered here
by high winds or high water,
and they put down roots so deep
that they became the identity of this place—
but few locals now know the name
of this stream, and its seasonal rise
wears away the course of the past;
yet I remain, misshapen by my seeking
of fissures, by my grasping of stones,
becoming the contours of resistance,
the contortions of my resilience,
holding in place what little remains
of a soil that once held me secure.

The Family, Circa 1919

The people who live in the Ozark country
of Missouri and Arkansas were, until very
recently, the most deliberately unprogres-
sive people in the United States.
                    —Vance Randolph
                    Ozarks Superstitions, 1947

In this photograph the old folks
and assorted cousins stand aligned
in front of their two-story farm house
with its tattered porch and wooden shingles.
The men sport stereotypical slouch hats
and the women wear aprons and sternness.
At one end of the line, great-Grandmother,
probably called away from her cookstove
for the nonsense of this photograph,
folds her arms to hide the glove
pot holder on her left hand.
At the other end of the line, squarely
facing the camera as though peacefully
surrendering to the firing squad
he is storied to have served
in as a Confederate soldier,
stands great, great-Grandfather,
bow legged, long armed, and widowed
in overalls and a white beard.
Near the center, is a great uncle
just home from World War I, in a dark,
pin-striped suit and military straightness,
his stare focused upon the hills beyond
the camera, having seen enough of the world
and its testing fields of progress.

The Family, Circa 1919

From the Great War

He returned to his parents'
farm in May of Nineteen
with nothing to discuss
and fell silently to building
a brooder house, a barn,
another brooder house,
banging away day upon day,
driving echoes deep into the hills
to bury distant echoes
he wanted no one else to hear.

Mayapple

Podophyllum peltatum

> *Despite its name, the plant blooms in March in the Ozarks (farther north it blooms in May); furthermore, it is not an apple but a member of the barberry family.*
> —Richard Rhodes
> *The Ozarks*

Perhaps the locals
got it wrong,
but the Mayapple
was known
not for beauty,
but for use,
not for bloom,
but for fruit.
Blossoming in March,
it bears in May
that which
only those who
have gathered it
in a past
of need and delight
and memory
can now know;
and when it ripened,
sweet and butter yellow,
so early after winter,
and long before melons
or blackberries,
it was an apple.

Hollyhocks

They still gather beside the well,
those old farm women,
although the rope and bucket
have been gone for years.
Wearing their brightest summer bonnets—
red, white, pink, and yellow—
they listen for the old men
working in the empty fields,
chatter about the weather,
nod their heads in the dry breeze,
and occasionally lean over the well
as if to glance at themselves
reflected against the vacant sky.

Family Photograph

Gathered on the front sidewalk,
after Christmas dinner and gifts,
we—brothers, sisters, cousins,
uncles, aunts, and in-laws—
posed for Grandma's box camera,
squinting into bitter December sun.
Four decades later our impatience
with one another shadows deeper
into our faces as she repeated,
with her head bowed to focus,
"Closer together, get closer together."

Age Four, Watching Mother Draw Water

It was a common well bucket,
like a section of slim stove pipe,
but crimped and tapered on both ends,
dull gray and galvanized,
as she lowered it into the well casing.
At the tug of its filled weight,
she began to pull, slowly, hand over hand,
and the rope grew taut, the pulley quiet,
as the twisted, knobby rope rose
and the bucket bumped the casing's sides;
then the rope grew wet
and the great mouth emerged,
black and round, gasping at the sky;
the long, lean body wet and sleek
and flecked with gray, silver, and rust,
with water gushing from its gills,
dripping from its tail; yet it was docile
as though stunned by this world,
and she held the rope at her hip
with her locked left arm
and reached with her strong right,
gripped the bucket by its jaw,
and, without ceremony or hesitation,
emptied its life into her water can.

School Yearbook

That October afternoon the District's
photographer interrupted science hour:
"Boys, show me what you do at recess."

And, boy, did we have something for him.
We had been cracking and eating walnuts
under a tree beside the baseball field;
this was a men's club, a hunter
and gatherer society, a sacred
communion, a last supper.

It was a last supper of sorts,
for this was our final year at our little school.
We were graduating into junior high
and would be bused to the consolidated
at the county seat the next year to be lost
among hundreds of strangers.

In spring the yearbooks arrived;
we turned to the faces
of future classmates; they stared
at us without acknowledgement,
and we studied the photographs
of them building science projects,
selecting books at their new library,
playing in the school band,
raising hands with ready answers.
Then we turned to ourselves, relegated
to two back pages; only one
photograph captured our activities:
a pack of boys crawling on all fours
in the tall fall grass grubbing
about the ground, some with dirty fingers
to their mouths, and some with arms
lifted high above their heads
grasping stones.

Elderly Bachelor on the Family Farm, Winter 1961

"The world must be made safe for democracy."
—President Woodrow Wilson
April 2, 1917

Another night of sub-zero predicted;
I've sealed off the extra rooms—
the bedroom and the kitchen—
and sleep and cook in the living room.
It's only me here; my parents
and little brother have been gone
several years, and my nephew
now has a farm over in the next county.
Today I drew a bucket of well water,
fed the chickens, brought a jar of green beans
from the root cellar, shoveled snow
from the front walk, and carried
in night's wood. No mail came.
This evening I'll crack black walnuts,
pick out their hearts, and throw the shells
into the fire. Then I'll study an old map
of Europe and re-trace the steps
I took under General Pershing
when my world was growing large
and needed me to save it.

The Names of Old Farmers

An argument for oral history

They often recollected economic depression
and world war and record droughts,
and remembered us and our parents
as children. We sometimes recall them—
soiled sweat of straw hats, long-sleeved
shirts in mid-summer, the scent
of Prince Albert or Velvet tobacco,
an occasional flash of a maimed finger—
and their eccentricities—one never wore
socks, one played piano only when alone,
another refused to learn to drive.
We sometimes say their names when telling
their stories—Bert Rambo, Gleamon Burtin,
Ruel Gann—as though mere names preserve
the depth of their past—Willie Matthews,
Venice Harris, Ray Elliot, George Fisher—
and upon hearing their names they rise
from the cemeteries of our minds
to stand tall before us once more and banter
with the children we once were, perhaps
offering to pull that tooth with pliers
or to trim our ears with a Barlow,
or they may give us some loose change
or a Moon Pie or a grape Nesbitt's,
and as in life, they begin to unfold
another story, but they soon fall silent,
puzzled by having now nothing to remember.

A Lone Loafer in Front of a Discount Store in Northwest Arkansas, Circa 1975

He held the dubious honor of living
longer than all of his old friends
and paused to be photographed
in that state.
　　　He crossed his legs
and leaned forward, resting his right
elbow on his crossed left knee, to stare directly
into the camera. He willed his every detail,
the stripes of his short-sleeved dress shirt,
the bib of his overalls, and the windrows
of his corduroy hat, into sharp focus.

Behind him the store window reflects
the blinding sunlight from the parking lot,
and the glare of the day is framed
in his old-fashioned eye glasses,
but in that moment his stare meet ours
and we see him and not the proverbial
comic, carefree whittler. He folded
that image away with the pocketknife
he almost conceals in his clenched hand.

A Lone Loafer
Photograph by David Bell

A Neighbor Woman

She knew long before the doctors,
but they knew too late.
She seemed to lose weight,
but she said she had been busy.
At moments she seemed
distant from the present
or too absolute about the future,
and when she placed her hundreds
of salt and pepper shakers
on the community rummage sale,
priced to sell, we were certain.
They had belonged to her mother,
who brought them from the old
country: windmills, wooden shoes,
blackbirds on a bough, a plump farm wife,
carrying two milk pails,
salt and pepper, silent and proud.

Icarus in the Ozarks

A First-Generation Student of Flight

His older brother plows, the younger herds sheep,
and they ignore his flight and fall to keep
their words and thoughts their own, their eyes on earth.
One was first, one last, and his middle birth
won him little birthright or affection,
so he made his way on wit and invention;
but they were put off by his newfound wings,
and when Father retired to join his schemes,
they sensed a shift in silent relations
and felt reduced by town-bred education;
but he was not trying to rise above
them, or change or escape the hills they love.
His dream was expressed in his drowning shout:
he sought something they could all talk about.

Three Boys Holding Coonhound Pups, Arkansas Ozarks, Circa 1975

Asked by the photographer to show
off their pups, the boys comply without a smile
and stand framed by a ramshackle barn
and thinning woods. The tall, lanky
boy in the center, the bill of his one-size-fits all
broader than his face, cradles four pups
in his arms and stares confidently
into the camera as if he understands why
he is being photographed. To the right,
a short, round-faced lad, with black
hair and dark eyes, wears a wide-brimmed,
unshaped cowboy hat and offers the two
pups in his arms with visible fear
that the camera may harm them. The third boy,
on the far left, stands a pace behind, half
hidden by the boy in center and slightly out
of focus. His empty arms are crossed;
he holds a only a flat, open-mouthed
expression as he squints into the sun.
Without a dog, he has no reason to be
in the photo—but finds no reason to step aside.

Three Boys Holding Coonhound Pups, Arkansas Ozarks, Circa
1975
Photograph by David Bell

The Living Room

My grandmother had three
daughters (my mother
was the middle one)
and six sons, and Uncle
Sam provided three wars
for the boys. Five went and four
came home, the other one
was shot through the heart
by a North Korean sniper
while eating lunch.
Grandmother's living
room had a darkened
corner where photographs
of farm boys in stiff military dress
hung upon the wall or stood
at attention on the black,
upright piano whose
keyboard was always locked.
My cousins and I avoided
this part of the house,
and Mother, who wanted
no darkened corners,
told us to never play army.

September Garden

I have planted my fall garden
twice—lettuce, beans, and spinach—
but a month of clouds prompted
only meek, scattered leaves
among a carpet of hardy weeds.
Grandma was a skilled gardener,
a mother of four during the Depression
and a widow for forty-six years,
so her garden had to produce,
so her hands had to grow strong
and her pleasures and affections distant.
I came to gardening too late, at midlife,
fourteen years after her death,
yet she and I cart steaming compost
and spade it into the soil,
turning up a prodigal potato
of the breed that always saw her through,
scarred by my pitchfork weeks earlier,
and a renegade onion sprouting blades
of infant green, and we slip them
into our pockets for an evening meal.

Sawmill

At the controls the man
pulls a lever gauging the cut
then pulls another forcing
the log into the whirling blade.
A sweet, fermented scent rises
and sawdust swarms like bees,
stinging the sweaty face
and arms of his son—
a lad just shy of being a man—
whose awkward shadow falls
across the blur of teeth
as he lifts each board away.
At the house the mother
fixes lunch, folds laundry, sweeps.
Each time the mill roars
and screams into a log,
her hands stumble in their work.

Opossum

It comes at night to pilfer
my back lawn
for a potato peel or heel
of tomato or for corn
wasted by red squirrels.
There is a primitive ugliness
about its busy nose,
tatty ears, reptilian tail,
and gray, ratty fur.
An obstinate beggar,
the dogs ignore it now
as I rattle the doorknob
to send it scurrying
back to darkness,
leaving only a footprint,
like a small, deformed hand,
in the damp earth.

Mayflies in the Foyer of a Nursing Home

Having fulfilled their duty to the species,
they arrive in this artificial world,
this sterile fluorescence,
where, on four fragile lacy wings
they bump against concrete walls,
flutter in lemon-scented confusion,
until they sit still,
drawn into themselves, comatose.
We feel a slight embarrassment in their presence
and cannot imagine their former lives—
hatching from eggs laid in water,
gulping life through gills,
feeding upon water plants—
but they have slipped those skins
to become subimago, sub-adults
without mouth or stomach,
bereft of voice and appetite.
Entomologists believe them the only insects,
perhaps the only living beings,
to undergo this stage of metamorphosis.

Tripod

She appeared in most of the family photographs
as a shadow, a silhouette holding the camera,
her torso and arms the tripod, as she captured
a lifetime of moments: her husband cross
armed in front of their first house or leaning
on their first car, him holding their first son,
birthdays, the boys' first days of school,
the new bicycles, stringers of fish, baseball games,
the boys' first cars, prom dates at the gate,
graduation gowns, military uniforms, automobiles
proclaiming "just married," everyone waving
good-bye; and then flowerbeds, him sitting
on the lawnmower or in the lawn chair,
the one vacation the two took together,
him shoveling snow or petting the old cat,
the last photograph of the house, then
the apartment in town, him waving
from a wheelchair, and her long shadow
stretching upon the ground
beside a flower-strewn grave
in a photograph containing no one.

The Fencerow

The history of his farm
is chronicled in this fencerow
where remnants of ancient white oak
posts—posts he split when he
was young and too poor
to afford any other—
hang gray and shrunken
held by rusted steeples
to brittle two-barbed wire.
Others, added a decade later
and split by a young neighbor
who had a family and needed work,
have also rotted from the ground.
Steel posts mark his mid-life,
when he could afford them
and was thinking ahead to the day
he could no longer walk the line
and drive posts. Five strands
of heavy gauge barbed wire
were also stretched then,
and even now they have the polish
of galvanization upon them;
then came death along the fencerow,
and the sumac returned,
and multi-flora rose, and the cedars,
some of which are now thicker
than his arms when he died.

The Fencerow

At an Estate Sale

This elderly lady, and then her things,
became too much for her adult children
to manage, so here is her art box
filled with tubes of acrylic paint;
she has pressed and squeezed
the bright and hopeful colors—
the cadmium yellow, dioxazine purple,
alizarin crimson, emerald green—
until they are bent beyond giving,
and on her easel's shelf the drippings
and smudges of these create
an abstract flower garden,
among whose eccentric petals
lie gray and blue smatterings
of a sky she knew was falling.

A Shelf of Old Hammers

They had their heads knocked
hard for too many years
as they spent life giving
and receiving pain;
with every blow they landed,
one was taken,
and now they have scarred,
blunted faces;
some hold their heads
slightly askew as though
still reeling from a hit,
and others have splintered
limbs wrapped in tape
worn thin and shabby;
and though beaten and maimed,
the ball-peen hammers
still flaunt their heft of pride,
and the claw hammers still pin
their ears back in anger.

Death of a Country Store

The store,
once a neighbor,
a friend,
who had been engaged
in the trade of life,
fell ill;
and when we were told
its diagnosis, we withdrew—
to grant privacy,
to avoid its gasps
when life support ended—
and now we pass
by without glancing,
for its corpse is still there,
the eyes wide open.

Two: A Smothering Embrace

Abandoned Barn

We have been absent
too long,
and it has fallen

into nostalgia
and obsolescence.
It's too late
to mend the roof
or re-hang the doors,

and the loft
will no longer hold
our weight.

Ancient lessons
announced in the rock
foundation, the axe-

hewn timbers, the knot
in the hay lift's rope,
and the derelict pitchfork,

seem old-
fashioned and quaint:

Store against tomorrow,
reap within reason,
return to the soil
more than was taken.

A sheet of tin
roofing rises and falls
in the wind.

Abandoned Barn

The View from My Bathroom Window

One hundred yards across the pasture,
a highway, then a convenience store,
a row of trees, and the Boston Mountains
beyond and beyond.

July is rolling in the fields,
the humidity plummeted
after yesterday's thunderstorm;
the sky is bluer than any crayon,
the air is September; this is a day
we cannot equal.

A cashier steps out the back door,
blocks it open with his right foot,
lights a cigarette, and blows smoke
away from the building. He studies
the fuel tanks and trash dumpsters,
watches the white dust rise from the chat
parking lot, ignores the traffic roar—
then he flips away the half cigarette
and steps in.

A Pear Tree in a Pasture near the Bisection of Two Scenic Byways

The final remnant
of an old home-
steader's orchard,
its produce is,
like a potato,
common and brown.
Most have lost
their taste for it,
and it blossomed
unnoticed this spring,
a local girl,
sincere and plain,
with a pedigree
of survival,
offering only
the forgotten fruit
of necessity.

A Fire Hydrant in an Annexed Pasture

The Herefords approach
hesitantly, stretching necks
and flaring nostrils, to investigate
the red-faced, pig-nosed man
who wears a red hard hat
and holds his stubby arms
outstretched at his sides
as though measuring the horizon
or presenting himself as a god.

The Last Ozarks Farmer

> *And whosoever shall not receive you, nor hear your words, when ye depart out of that house or city, shake off the dust of your feet.*
>
> *Matthew 10:14*

He looks around him at the urban sprawl
And shakes the dust from ancient overalls.

A Local Fable

> *And, since it is the undoubted preference*
> *of many to remain in the vicinity of the*
> *place of their birth, ... the people re-*
> *mained in the poverty which heaven had*
> *decreed for them.*
> —John Kenneth Galbraith
> *The Affluent Society*

> *Pale: 1. A stake or pointed stick; picket.*
> *2. Archaic. A fence enclosing an area. 3.*
> *The area enclosed by a fence or boundary.*
> —*The American Heritage Dictionary.*

A crow walked across a field of snow,
and the snow melted a little by day
and froze again by night,
causing the tracks to grow large
and grotesque until discovered
by the children of the village,
who then told of a gigantic, clawed
beast prowling beyond the pale,
and the elders said nothing to dissuade them
and half wished to believe it themselves.

Megahertz

When the local radio station in the valley
increased its wattage, folks living on the ridge
near its tower experienced electromagnetic
disruption. The morning obituaries, sponsored
by Myers-Wilson Funeral Home, where they treat
you like a member of the family, came out
of their coffeemakers. Although disconcerted
at first (the ashes and dust made the coffee
too black), these practical folks soon adjusted
to drinking coffee with the professional, detached
voice announcing death. Sometimes they
recognized a name and decided against
a second lump of sugar or dash of cream
and stirred their Joe staring into its steam
or watching the few grounds in their cups
circling like miniscule turkey buzzards.
They also took all in stride when *Community Calendar*
cut in on soap operas: the promiscuous blonde
(who is undergoing a transformation from villain
to victim) embraces her best friend's husband,
nibbles his ear lobe and breathes into his mind,
"There will be a chili supper Friday night
at 7:00 sponsored by the First Baptist Church."
The man rubs her shoulders, levels his reassuring
eyes deep into hers and replies, "Bingo
has been cancelled tonight at the VFW,"
and they confidently step away from one
another just as Wifey-Poo enters the café.
These viewers found this entertaining and post-
modern, but after a few weeks, they grew heavy
and dull, for after they had closed the chicken
house door for the night, locked their own doors,
turned out the lights, and laid down
to sleep, instead of hearing a coyote howling
in a far-off hollow, or the wind blowing
through trees, or the silence of the stars,
they heard, coming out of the coil springs

of their mattresses, the tinny voice of civilization
afraid and trembling, playing old songs,
taking the next caller, sifting the latest news,
as it tried to make it through the coming night.

Rain Crow

My ancestors believed
they knew when
rains would come
and spent hours talking
in their doorways
about the weather,
filling woods
with hoots and coos
of divination, but
that skill is now
dismissed as folklore
and the sky grows ever
more unpredictable,
so now no one listens to
or knows how to interpret
my cries of bewildered error.

The Heirs

My father attended farm auctions
and rescued his old neighbors'
tools from becoming anonymous
in flea markets, and on the occasions
of Christmas or birthday
he would draw one from his collection
as a gift to me, wrapping it
in an oral reminder of its original owner,
and as I dig this posthole
with a crow bar he passed to me,
Dad, gone now ten years,
and old man Harris, gone twenty more,
walk the fencerow together,
trying the firmness of my posts
and thumbing the tautness of my wire.

Condemned

> *Lester [age 86] clearly valued land above*
> *money.   In the past few years he has*
> *turned down several lucrative offers for*
> *his hundred acres, half of which now lie*
> *condemned for a planned Branson by-*
> *pass.*
>
> —Lisa Moore LaRoe
> "Ozark Harmony"
> *National Geographic*, April 1998

Each year millions make the pilgrimage
and pay their retired dollars
seeking a version of the region
as it never existed. They and their idols
are not satisfied to step around Lester,
an old farmer of memories,
for their bliss is threatened by the dissent
of one man. They cannot profit from him,
so they grant him no value,
but they make his land valuable
and exercise their blighted
right to possess. Then they sacrifice
the farm to the gods of costumed progress,
predigested distraction, and yuk-yuk jokes
at the altar standing in the pasture
near the side of the highway: bathed
in florescence the forty-foot image
of a man wearing a sequined suit
of wagon wheels and fringes
stands among the faded stars, flashing
whitened teeth over the condemned hills.

On a Bluff Overlooking the Buffalo National River

Few monuments commemorate
those who lost home
to treaty, poverty, or law—
but they would refuse
any memorial offered
by those who take
and do not understand the loss,
so perhaps this ancient cedar
standing in its crucible
of stone, wind, and sky
high above the river
is the most fitting marker
as it spins ring
upon ring of thin years
around its knotted heart.

On a Bluff Overlooking the Buffalo National River

Whip-Poor-Will

Folklorists report that it was believed
to be the call of death, but we never
held such superstitions and welcomed it
when it came to call at dusk.
Beginning its chant in the shadows
of woods, it would flutter closer
to continue its vigil in the path
leading from the back porch to the barn,
and I would lie awake and watch
shadows of the walnut leaves
on the wall and listen to the slow
breath of my sleeping brother
and to my parents talking each other
to sleep, and then I would drift off
wrapped in the belief that it would be forever
before any of that life would pass away.

Three: A Sense of Place

Homestead on Federal Land

They have been gone forty years—
forced out by eminent domain—
but their absence pulls
weathered boards from the barn
and clapboards from the house,
wrenches gates off hinges,
pushes foundation stones out of plumb,
and occasionally drops a window
glass or tears wall paper.
A path leads to the front lawn,
the broad, shaded porch invites,
and both front doors are always open,
but we should never believe
that we are still welcome.

Homestead on Federal Land

A New Arrival Becomes a Rural Correspondent for the Local Newspaper

He moved here to get away from it all
and to have time to write,
but he had nothing to write
and became a correspondent for the *Daily*.
He bought the old Wilkerson place
and renamed it Nature's Haven Ranch
and his scattered neighbors
the Bear Ridge Community.
He shows his outsider foolishness
in surprising ways—he cuts hedge trees
for firewood and black oaks for corner posts
and plants his garden near roots of walnut trees;
he knocks on the wrong door
when he comes to visit, visits
once each week just before his deadline,
and latches the gate wrong when he leaves.
But he records his neighbors' lives with style
and confidence as he places people
in the same sentence who have silently agreed
never to appear in the same sentence
or on the same side of the mountain:
he admires what folks don't want to share,
advertizes what they wish to keep to themselves,
tells what they had for Sunday dinner,
tramps across unmarked graves of the heart,
taps old ghosts on the shoulder,
and names things by strange names—
all with flawless grammar and punctuation.
He writes that his "adopted home" is "nestled"
and "quaint," incessantly points
out himself as being a "furriner,"
and notes his delight at every folk adage or scrap
of dialect; yet he remains unaware
that he need not remind the neighbors
that he doesn't belong:

he may never realize that their lives,
like the chipped gravy bowl on the high shelf,
or the worn Winchester above the door,
are not there to be on display,
but to be out of reach.

Small Bluets

Hedyotis crassifloia

We find them blinking new-born
eyes in March long before we
have thought to dream
of flowers. The closer we
look, the tinier they become
until each of their four
pointed petals is smaller
than a vole's nose. We
spade up a handful of soil
containing a blue colony
and place them in a jar lid
on the window sill
above the kitchen sink
from where they,
a native and wild bonsai,
pull the rest of life
into the correct proportions.

Bloodroot

Sanguinaria canadensis

It prefers the moist, lower slopes
of rocky, wooded hillsides;
suspicious and tight-lipped,
it offers a single blossom
for only one day,
white and daisy-like,
and then remains a single leaf
wedged low out of the earth,
hiding its joy among ground cover,
but throbbing from root tip
to leaf tip with blood
drawn from the thin soil
to which it clings.

Wild Strawberries

In the cemetery,
they grow low to the ground
to avoid the mower's blade,
and after Sunday services
children search among tombstones
of strangely named ancestors
collecting the small, ripened hearts
until parents call them away,
and then they come racing
through the gate—the last
one through has to latch it—
as they lick the earthy juices
of childhood from their fingers.

Without Warning, Summer

"The sun turns back . . . retraces its course . . . ."
—David Ames Wells
Familiar Science, 1856

Without warning, summer
began its long death;
now the sun leans ever southward,
casting, with a melancholy difference,
shadows it has cast before.

Young barn swallows
dive to catch and release, again
and again, thistledown.

Wind from a distant rainstorm
spirals yellowed walnut leaves
to fill the lawn as dandelions
did only weeks before.

Our house dog, out for a romp,
chases a dragonfly,
causing it to careen
through the woven wire fence;

stymied, the dog can only watch it go,
puzzled by its departure,
ignorant of its being.

Nursing Home

> from her wheelchair
> she watches
> graceful goldfish

> > he once farmed
> > 400 acres, but now
> > this geranium

143B cries
she cannot remember
her daughter's name

> jigsaw puzzle;
> each piece
> a piece of time

> > her calendar
> > compliments of
> > the local funeral home

> birthday balloons
> tied to his wheelchair
> everyday

her son visits;
he glances repeatedly
at his watch

Nocturnal Visitors

(A Widow's Lament)

The yellow Labrador died in her sleep
of old age last week. She passed
in her favorite place, a hole
she had dug in the soft dirt
under the manure spreader parked
in the shed. Now the wild comes closer
each night. First it was a possum,
rattling the cats' pan on the back step,
licking away whatever had accumulated.
Then a skunk, fearless and dainty;
and tonight, as I stand in my darkened house
watching by porch light, three adolescent
raccoons arrive. Finding nothing
in the food dish, they sniff my tracks
leading from the wash house and peep
through the crack under my storm door.
Growing bored, these young toughs shove
and punch one another; one seems to hold
a Zippo to another's butt, and the three
tumble together wrestling with quickened
chatter. Then they pause suddenly alert
and immediately refit their masks.
They throw a destructive glance at my mailbox
and try the latches of all the outbuildings.
I don't recognize any of them, although
I have probably met their parents in passing.
I hope that some night when they smell
death under my door, they find
the manners not to ring the doorbell
before they run into the woods laughing.

A Grove of White Poplars

Populus alba

In a pasture far from the road
no remnants of outbuildings
or of the house remain,
only a copse of trees,
trees not native to this soil
and that were probably planted
by an early settler to remind her
of home back east and that took root
though the family did not.
Even when I was young,
the old folks could not recall
when a family had ever lived there
or where or why they had gone,
but the wind seemed to always stir
in that grove, turning its leaves
to reveal undersides as white
as the crests of tides
far from that land-locked farm.

Two-Story Farmhouse beside Arkansas 62

Finding the bare,
dilapidated clapboards,
rusted roof, and missing
doors and windows
picturesque, passersby pull
over to photograph
their discovery,
but upon the appearance
of these intruders,
the old house,
like the furry gray
and black spider
in its cupboard, pauses,
backs into shadows,
tucks in legs and pedipalps,
and fills its many eyes
with absence.

Two-Story Farmhouse beside Arkansas 62

A Hill Cemetery

> *The Ozark Center has had few prizes to*
> *stimulate the ambition of its people, most*
> *of whom have lived uneventful lives and*
> *therefore made little local history.*
> —Carl O. Sauer
> *Geographic Missouri,* 1920

After only a mile, the trail
terminates at the cemetery,
and the four of us drift
apart reading tombstones.

Freed from her ubiquitous leash
and cheered by laughter and praise,
our small dog races from master to master
on a blur of stumbling, stubby legs.

Occasionally one of us shouts
to report an inscription:
An ancient date, an aphorism,
or an eternal warning
fading from stone.

The sun grows, the dog tires;
we gravitate to the shade, and there,
in this oldest section, beside the parents,
lie five small stones, each
bearing only a name and brief date
to note these infant, uneventful lives.

Barn Loft

Through vertical chinks, late
        summer sun enters white

and broken by oak limbs
        and slants upon the wind-

swept floor. The smell of dry-rotting
        timbers is the only harvest.

The doors, wired shut, sag
        upon the rust of hinges.

Ladder rungs are grooved
        and worn smooth by work

boots and working hands
        that rest among the shadows.

Hand-Dug Well

Electricity and indoor plumbing
arrived late in these hills,
and in many lawns old wells remain,
framed by rock walls, thigh high
and capped with a great stone.
They became obsolete, then monuments,
and are now only obstacles to mowing.
Today we lifted away the capstone
and peered into the depths looking
for something we do not know
and saw only the stones of the inner wall
stacked downward into darkness
and the reflection of ourselves
with hands cupped around eyes,
like a family pressing their faces
to the window of a house
they have locked themselves out of.

Hand-Dug Well

Crosscut Saws

You see these old men
in most every flea market
here in the hills. They were found
hiding in the wood shed
or barn loft or abandoned
chicken house where they wandered
off to when they became obsolete,
and now they are only a surface
on which to paint an idealized past—
a cabin too close to a river,
a mailbox filled with flowers,
geese wearing ribbons.
Reduced to mere decoration,
they are almost unrecognizable
as what they once were.

Sage Bush

Started from the plant
Mother grew from her father's,
my sage bush was the sole survivor
in my garden during the recent drought.
Grasshoppers, having no choice
in the burnt fields, chewed
the edges of its evergreen leaves,
but now, revived by fall rains,
it steps forward in ragged pride,
with holes in the elbows of its work shirt
and patches on its knees.

A Grasshopper Who Lived in My House during the Recent Drought

He must have stolen inside
clinging to the underbelly of a bath towel
brought from the clothesline.
Shorn of his natural habitat
he tried to conceal himself
on the floral couch pillow,
on the shadowed side of the TV remote,
or on the backside of a floor lamp,
but when roused from hiding,
he kicked his heels at the air,
gesticulating with his four front legs
and spitting tobacco juice
amid shrieks of my daughters.
But they grew accustomed to him,
for he became careful to sit in plain sight
to avoid startling the natives,
and after a time we regarded him
to be a lost and unfortunate traveler,
like a lone sailor blown off course,
yet we harbored some suspicions,
as more and more of his people
affixed themselves to the screened windows,
that perhaps it was his duty to unbolt
the door in the middle of the night.
Then, one morning, he was gone;
we looked in all the usual places,
but we never found him.
He may have hitched a ride out
on the cuff of my trousers;
more likely, deprived of the morning dew
and fresh leaves, he grew weak
and crawled into a shadowed nook
where he forgot that the only summer
of his life was a drought
and dreamed about the sweet clover
of which his mother once sang.

Arkansas Tourist Town in Winter

A sign boasts
of the small population,
but most of the 35
have gone
to their real homes
for the winter,
leaving a regiment
of crows to tend
the dormant grass
of the town park.
The store, café, and canoe
rental are closed
for the season;
only the streets
and river are open.
Fiberglass canoes, yellow,
red, forest green,
lie silent on trailers,
their backs to the sealed sky.
A yellow, diamond-
shaped sign
continues to warn
out of season,
"Watch Out For Children."
Another sign,
encased in Plexiglas,
recites the town's history—
how the railroad
came to town
around the turn
of the century and left
by mid-century
with most
of the timber
and young folks—
the only history the town has
or may now ever have.

Crossroads Town in Rural Arkansas

Main Street, the main road out,
ambles over railroad tracks,
the only intersection folks take note of,
before narrowing into the distance
and fading into blue of falling snow.
The X of the crossing sign
prompts many to cross their hearts
and swear they will never come back,
and from this angle the mortar lines
of the empty brick store fronts,
their porch rafters, and even the corrugation
of the sheet metal, point the way out of town.
The only thing that seems to suggest staying
are the snowflakes, the size of overcoat buttons,
drifting into town with a slow swagger
before they melt upon contact.

Pleasant Hill Cemetery

They pull off
the new four-lane
and into the cemetery's
circular drive;
braking suddenly,
the two step out to stretch
and to let their dog
do her business.
They distract themselves
with old gravestones,
laughing
and mispronouncing
some local names.
Then they congratulate
the dog,
and hurry into traffic,
happy to have found
a grassy place
where no one cares.

Farm Journal: Haiku Sequence

out of the city,   surprised by the sound   of my footsteps

barn door—   opening and closing   for the wind

old pony—   breath frozen white   in whiskers

walking back,   my old snowprints   belong to a stranger

falling through   the barn roof,   stars and moon

shifting fog,   a crow fades   his call remains

heron and I   standing   still

new moon,   fish share their pond   with every star

wild ivy,   after cutting it for years   she lets it grow

snake in the shed,   her garden tools lie   in the rain

bullfrog,   with each breath   summer deepens

heat wave—   even the concrete chickens   stand in the shade

setting early   in the cracked window   late summer sun

in my mailbox   again today   only that same brown leaf

i turn out my lamp   the moon jumps   through my window

Farm Machinery

According to the identification plate,
it was a Papec Hay Chopper and Silo Filler
sitting obsolete and broken
near the edge my childhood's pasture.
Forty years later it still sits there, a world
of spouts, chains, pulleys, levers,
rollers, and chutes that pitched
among the white caps of the North Atlantic,
rigging heavy with ice, shouts
of warning from the crow's nest,
all hands to battle stations, cannons blazing;
or buzzed the skies of Britain,
the dread of the Luftwaffe, banking
and looping like a barn swallow;
or submerged in the deep Pacific,
holding its breath and filling its ballast tanks,
its periscope up and torpedoes
racing toward the barn;
or a lone Sherman charging through trees
to blast the lines of hay-bale Panzers
falling out of formation on the French countryside.
Even now, when I pull this lever,
breaking the rust that almost binds it,
the wind rises in the trees,
and the birds alight and tremble.

Four: Poems, My Father

"Sundays too my father got up early . . . ."

Robert Hayden

"Those Winter Sundays"

Bicycle

On the backside my grandmother
long ago wrote *Probably 13.*
On the other side, my father, a boy
on his bicycle, stands outside
the back porch of his childhood.
Like Wyeth's lad in *Young America*
he is drastically off center,
almost to exit stage right
as he holds his machine broadside
and faces the morning sun
with his head tilted
slightly downward to shade his eyes;
behind him in the shadows of the screened
porch are his little sister and mother,
and holding the camera is perhaps
his older sister home from college,
or his father, who at that moment
had only two years to live.
Dad stands gripping the handle bars
with both hands and has one foot
on the pedals as he speeds
out of the frame of boyhood.

Bicycle

The Phillipsburg Panthers Yearbook, 1952-53

In the heat of the game,
wearing black trunks and jersey
without name or number,
he is shooting a free throw
in the dimly lit gymnasium.
His form would rile
the most stoic of coaches:
pushing the ball with both
hands and watching its flight
rather than focusing on the vacuum
within the metal rim.
An opponent, dressed in white,
arms akimbo, stands behind him
beyond the range of the flash,
and a referee, whistle in mouth,
leans forward to watch the battle
for the possible rebound—
but in this moment
Dad's arms are stretched upward,
his two thick hands,
which readily grasped any work
and released all when done,
are lifted and opened wide;
the ball is suspended in its ascent,
and in this frame
there is no net, no scoreboard,
only the joy of the toss.

The Phillipsburg Panthers Yearbook, 1952-53

Jigsaw Puzzle

Only during that winter storm
did you take time from laboring;
we milked and fed the cows
and then the cold and snow kept us
indoors piecing together a jigsaw puzzle,
a photograph of an aristocratic garden
with manicured beds of tulips,
a bridge over a plotted stream,
a three-tiered fountain with cherubs
pouring wine from concrete vases,
but as with so many of our projects—
the odd-shaped boards produced by
our worn sawmill, the heifers
whose udders mysteriously dried away,
the hogs that died in the sun—
a piece was missing near the center,
but we glued and framed it, allowing
that jigsaw pothole in the cobblestones
to trouble all fine folks who loitered there.

Paces

Dad was always stepping things off.
Although he was only five feet six,
two of his paces were six feet even.
He stepped off acres of ground,
spaces between fence posts
dimensions of a barn or garden spot,
but on that morning, he and I
stood beside a road on a windy hill,
where a neighbor boy had,
the night before, left the earth
at 110 miles per hour and flew
rolling through the air,
and Dad measured that flight:
24 paces, 72 feet.
I estimated the height of the mud
spattered on a nearby pole
with my eight-foot reach,
and he stared at me as though
I was a miracle grown tall beside him.

Dad's Old Ford Tractor

Low compression, low on water,
four deflating tires,
low on oil, out of gas,
the key a pair of pliers,
the steering's loose, the clutch grabs,
there's no bottom to the brakes,
the starter drags, the battery's dead,
but a push is all it takes,
so gas it up, and pop the clutch,
we'll fix it some other tomorrow—
it wasn't much, but was always there,
for anyone to borrow.

Retired

We persuaded him to sell
the cows he had milked twice
each day for life.

Now he sits late every
evening at the head
of the dinner table
reading an encyclopedia,

dozing with arms folded
over his chest,
waking to lift his eyes
to the empty chairs,
or to stare at the window,

hoping to recall some chore
left unfinished
beyond the darkened glass.

Death in June

Summer returns
      to his fields
without him.

His implements,
      exhausted by his will
to stay put,

to draw ecstatic
      life from this
forty acres of soil,

rust in his absence,
      sitting abandoned,
brown and shattered,

like a cicada
      shell broken open
by irrepressible song.

Death in June

Five: Requiem

The Morning Paper

A disaster, hundreds
of thousands thought dead;
another shooting, perhaps
the deadliest yet, but still
counting; banks posting
record losses, war promised
for another decade, Congress
investing in debt, a pandemic
predicted, sewage released
in a local stream, editorialists
squealing like rats in a barrel,
important games are won
and lost, the cartoonists see nothing
funny and repeat it,
housing prices rebound,
but thousands are homeless;
the obituaries are filled
with people our own age.
All this is rolled tight,
shaped like a racing baton,
and lies on my street curb,
as if dropped there by a runner
who believed the race had been lost.

When the Barn was Red

An old barn, faded gray and weather-worn
has lost it paint and roof to sun and storm.

A little boy questions Sister first,
"Do you remember when the barn was red?"

"The barn was never red, and I should know,
for two months from now, I'll be ten years old."

He turned to Mother, busy at her chores,
"Do you remember when the barn was red?"

"It was gray the day I came in '68,
and your father has never found time to paint."

The little boy questions Father next,
"Do you remember when the barn was red?"

"The barn was never red when I was young,
now go and leave me be—my work's not done."

The little boy questions Grandpa last,
"Do you remember when the barn was red?"

"I'll sit and tell the story while you play,
for I painted the barn just yesterday."

A Workbench Built of Lumber Salvaged from My Late Father's Loft Barn

While working in my shop,
I sometimes hear rain on a tin roof
when no cloud is in the sky,
or hear calves rustling hay in mangers
or the steady breath of the milking compressor,
and I pause in my work, lift my goggles,
and turn my good ear to the sound
only to hear my neighbor mowing grass
or a school bus braking to a stop.
When sweeping, I find what appears
to be hay dust—maybe flecks of clover
and orchard grass—beneath the bench
as it once sifted through cracks
of the loft floor; each spring,
although doors and windows are screened,
shadows of swallows dive, fork tailed
and fearless, between the bench's legs
searching for adobe nests on ancestral rafters;
when I exit the shop, my father says,
from somewhere over my shoulder,
"Always, always latch the barn door."

In the Fields: A Rebuttal

"Each of these landlords walked amidst his fields
Saying, 'Tis mine . . . ."
—Ralph Waldo Emerson
"Hamatreya"

While working or playing in our fields,
Brother and I often unearthed
a rusted fragment—a broken blade,
a worn cog, a bit of chain—certain
to be a relic from the Civil War
or a wagon train—and carried it
to Dad, who, while asking where
we found it, would shift the artifact
from hand to hand and reach
across experience to place it again
in its original position on an archaic
implement—a horse-drawn plow,
a mowing machine, a corn planter—
and he would then hang it on the barn wall,
pleased to have been reassured
that he would never be alone in the fields.

About the Author

Phillip Howerton

Phillip Howerton was brought up on a small dairy farm in southern Dallas County, Missouri, and is a sixth-generation Ozarker. After spending several years as a milk truck driver, beef farmer, and production worker, he earned degrees in English, history, and education from Drury University and a doctorate in American literature and rhetoric and composition from University of Missouri-Columbia. His poems, photographs, and essays have appeared in wide variety of journals and books, and he has received grants from the Missouri Humanities Council, Arkansas Humanities Council, and the National Endowment for the Humanities. He is a co-founder and co-editor of *Cave Region Review* and an associate professor of English at Missouri State University-West Plains.

CPSIA information can be obtained
at www.ICGtesting.com
Printed in the USA
LVOW01s0515111115
461938LV00006B/21/P